DISCOVER LIGHT IN THE DARKNESS

Revelations of hope to guide you in a fallen world

Niel de Beer

Print on demand

ISBN: 978-0-620886-75-8

Cover design by: POD
Printed in the United States of America

It is during our darkest moments that we must focus to see the light

ARISTOTLE

CONTENTS

INTRODUCTION

What this book can do for you

"When you get into a tight place and everything goes against you, till it seems as though you could not hang on a minute longer, never give up then, for that is just the place and time that the tide will turn."

Harriet Beecher Stowe

Do you find yourself feeling hopeless? Do you need help to overcome fears and challenges in your life? Are you clueless about how to get rid of certain habits? Do you think that there is nothing you can do? From this book, you will learn how to overcome challenges, discover ways in which to create hope, master techniques necessary for successful living, and receive revelations that can change your outlook on life.

I wrote this book so that you can discover your true identity and purpose in life. And know that with God all things are possible even amid your darkest days. I really hope that this book will motivate you to live the life God intended for you. Someone famously said you don't have a problem you have a knowledge problem. The book of Hosea tells us people perish from a lack of knowledge. It goes on to say they perish because they rejected the knowledge. Sometimes what is missing in our lives is a piece of information we ought to know.

In the beginning, God created the heavens and the earth. Now the earth was formless and empty, darkness was over the surface of the deep, and the Spirit of God was hovering over the waters. And God said, "Let there be light," and there was light...

Genesis 1:1-3

PREFACE

"I may not be where I want to be, but thank God I am not where I used to be."

Joyce Meyer

This book was written because I want to give people hope, inspiration, and ultimately encourage them to put their faith in God. I have a passion for anything inspirational of nature as well as giving people hope. And so what motivated me through the writing process was the feedback I received from people. People telling me that I have a gift. With this book, I get to share my gift with the world, which is such an exciting thought.

My life changed in so many ways through the revelations and principles I am about to share with you. The wisdom and revelations in this book is a gift from God. A long time ago, I prayed for revelations of wisdom, and ever since that is exactly what God has been granting me with.

I always looked at my motivational heroes such as Zig

Ziglar, Les Brown, Jim Rohn and Ravi. I thought to myself, that is what I want to do. I want to inspire and motivate people. I want to speak to the masses and become an author too. And so I feel it's not just something I wished to pursue, but that it is also God's purpose for my life.

I encountered many stumbling blocks while writing - anything from self-doubt to the costs involved in making this book. But this book and the ideas in it have been a long time in the making. Not only is it a passion of mine but also a vision God gave me. So I simply had to do whatever it takes. I've had people stare straight through me as I told them I am writing a book. The vast majority of them thought I was making a joke. Only a few believed in me. But I knew God's belief in me would be the deciding factor.

So why am I the one to deliver this message? Because we each have a unique story and message that can change the world. Why do you need this book? Because it has the potential to change lives, and I know it will impact yours. Why should you not wait? Because life is a once off experience and you were called for a time such as this. This book can profoundly impact you and instill a sense of hope within you. Why this? Because the content of this book is God-ordained, God changed my life, and He can change yours too. Because the same God that made me, also made you.

ACKNOWLEDGEMENTS

I would like to acknowledge the following people for assisting me in the creation of this book: Maxine, Bianca and all the editors at Print on demand, thank you for your tireless efforts in making this book a reality. Also to my sponsors: Robbie, Peppe, Andries, Louwrens, Dad, Almero and Charl - without your financial assistance this book would not come to fruition. A big shout out to my wife for supporting me throughout the writing process, and last but not least to God for never giving up on me.

1. THERE'S LIGHT

God saw that the light was good and He separated the light from the darkness.

Genesis 1:4

The speed of light is approximately 300,000 kilometers per second – faster than anything else in the known universe. Light energy is also the only energy visible to the human eye. We are living in times where we are confronted with many tragedies. Anything from famine, natural disasters, viruses, and the list goes on. In times like these, we as God's children need to be the light. We need to be a message of hope in a world mostly devoid of it.

No matter how strong the light is, darkness is never far away. If you switch on the light, the whole room lights up instantaneously. However, the darkness is looming right outside, waiting for the lights to go out, so it can envelop the room. The light, therefore, needs to keep shining if it is to keep out the darkness.

"God did not create evil. Just as darkness is the absence of light, evil is the absence of God."

Albert Einstein

Whatever challenges you are facing, just remember that there is always light at the end of the tunnel. Things might seem impossible now, and a breakthrough looks unlikely, but there are things on Earth and in our lives that defy logic.

Every cell in your body gets replaced every couple of years. Therefore, you don't have the same body you had years ago. Likewise, you don't have to continue to be the same person you used to be. Isn't it strange that amid so many tragedies, both on Earth and in our lives, life carries on? It was designed that way. And whatever happens, you should keep moving because if you do, you will discover light in the darkness.

2. THE PROCESS

We live in a result-orientated world. If we do not see results right away, we assume that whatever we are doing is not working and we throw in the towel. Instant gratification, a get now and work later mentality, consumes us.

"If you want to give up remember, the result depends on the process… and not vice versa."

It takes five years for a Chinese bamboo tree to grow to a height of ninety feet, but the growth only happens in the last couple of weeks. For the greater part of five years, you will see no progress, yet it's preparing to shoot up. If within that time you stop nurturing it the tree will die. This is what happens to most people's dreams. We depend on results, proof, and things happening now! Little do we realize that the result depends on the task and that the process is the most important aspect. If we focus on the process and persevere, results will come naturally. It is the process that shapes you and ultimately brings forth success. The most important question you should ask yourself is, "Am I still busy with the activity?" The result does not make your dreams come true; the process does. Don't

rely on proof or results; rely on your ability to persevere.

> *"Your ability to succeed hinges on your ability
> to persevere."*

We must be stubborn in our approach to reach our goals and dreams. And keep faith that success will follow if we persevere. Also, remember just because you can't witness any progress doesn't mean there isn't any. I've never witnessed a butterfly develop inside a cocoon, yet it does. Failure will always be part of the equation, but it makes our successes in life even sweeter. However, failure does not mean anything if we don't learn from it and apply it to our future endeavors.

> *"Hindsight only has meaning if we use it for foresight."*

Hindsight is an exact science. If we can use past experiences to assist us with foresight, then it will enable us to become more successful in life. God created us to be all that we can be, not half, not three quarters, but everything we can be. So stick to the process, stay focused and you will make a success out of life!

3. THE INFLUENCER

There once were two guys, Jonathan and Peter, both of whom were quite good at shooting a bow and arrow. They were also competitive and would occasionally take each other on. One day they went to the target range and had a contest. The best out of three rounds would win. Unfortunately, the occasion got marred as Peter had the flu, which resulted in a lot of sneezing and blurry vision. However, he kept quiet about it as he didn't want to make excuses in case he lost. It became evident that if he were to win, he would have to perform a miracle.

As the contest progressed, Jonathan became better and better, but poor old Peter was getting worse. On one occasion, Peter aimed at the target, and just as he was about to release the arrow, a sudden gust of wind deterred his arrow, preventing him from getting a good shot. The very next go, while Jonathan was aiming, the wind died down, and he had a shot in near perfect conditions. Besides having the flu, Peter had to contend with all these other seemingly unfair circumstances. Needless to say, Peter lost quite badly. However, staying true to his word, he did not complain. But Jonathan did not hesitate to bring up Peter's unfortunate circumstances. He mentioned how Peter's sneezing, the gusts of wind, etc. harmed his performance, and had the conditions been more favorable, Peter would have performed much better. Jonathan realized that it was the adverse conditions that affected Peter's overall performance. Little did Jonathan know that his performance was also influenced by conditions, even though more favorable and considered to be the "norm".

In life, we are all influenced by someone or something. And depending on your outlook, conditions can either be normal or abnormal. Having the flu can seem strange to someone who has strong immunity, but to someone with weak immunity, it is entirely normal. Windy conditions feel abnormal to someone who mostly stays indoors and then experiences it when they go outside. While for someone who lives in a tent on a mountain top, the wind will be part of their everyday life. How can one then define normal if there are so many versions of it?

> *"Normal is an illusion. What is normal for
> the spider is chaos for the fly."*
>
> Charles Addams

When you decide to leave behind your old way of life and follow God, there will be people telling you that you have been brainwashed, that you are at a low point in life, that it is just a phase or that you need God as a crutch to make you feel better. They'll say that you are being influenced by people and things and that you ought not to listen to it. They'll try to make you believe that following God is not normal when in truth; it is just because it is not normal to them. Think about this for a moment – people and things also influenced them. They are also brainwashed, but because they share the mindset of the masses, it seems normal. We all are being influenced; the question is, by whom? Who or what is the primary influence in your life?

4. HABITS

"Habits are the outcome of repeated decisions. That starts manually and ends up automatically."

Habits are such powerful forces that have the potential to change our lives or destroy them. I used to spend my weekends drinking and smoking my life away. And changing the habit was tough. However, once I replaced it with something positive, like writing my book, and started doing that instead, it became automatic after a while. Be careful of what you get used to because you can get used to anything. Trying out new things might feel uncomfortable in the beginning but after repeatedly engaging in a particular activity, it will become your norm. The difference between using drugs once and using it daily is called habit. The foundation upon which a habit grows is a mindset of "one last time". I remember back in my drinking days I uttered those very words. It fools us into thinking the habit will die, when in fact, it is feeding the addiction.

In any pursuit to change a habit, there will be the temptation to compromise. But we simply cannot change for the better while still holding onto bad habits which bring us down. If something promises that we can have the best of both worlds, we should resist it.

"Compromise will initially make you do a little less. And ultimately make you do nothing at all."

If we want to get rid of a habit, we must first acknowledge that it is wrong. So many people don't shake a habit because they don't realize that it is a problem or many times they are waiting for the right time. Circumstances will never be ideal. They weren't ideal for you to start the habit, and they won't be ideal for you to end it. Act today and start something new, and bit by habit, things will change for you.

5. THE POWER OF POSITIVITY

To survive, you have to eat regularly. If you go without water long enough, you will also die. If you don't continually fill up your petrol tank, your car will standstill. One shower a week won't keep you clean. There are many things that we continually have to do, which should we neglect to do them, will no doubt adversely affect our lives.

"The power of positivity does not lie in what it is; its power lies in what it can do for you."

It is interesting how many people point out that positivity does not last when in fact so many things in our life do not last. We have to continually do them. So why should having a positive mindset be any different? People that are constantly negative think that being positive is somehow unattainable.

"The power of positivity is like a plane, it can fly without you, but if you want it to take you places, you need to book a flight."

What they fail to remember is that a negative mind-set also needs to be fed daily. Of course, it's not always easy to be positive and granted, negativity often comes more natural. However, making excuses as to why being positive is unachievable is not only wrong but also life-damaging. Life is hard and always being positive is a struggle. Nevertheless, don't let that turn positivity into a pie in the sky; rather make it something to reach for. Just because the ceiling is difficult to reach, does not mean it is unreachable. Sometimes all we need is a chair, and perhaps all you need is a different mindset. Positivity isn't only reserved for a select few, but for everyone who chooses to use it. Positivity flourishes without man's approval. So if you want positivity to work in your favor, you will need to use it.

6. THE WALLS ARE CLOSING IN

We've all had moments where we felt as though the walls were closing in on us. Nobody goes through life without these moments. Unfortunately, it is a harsh reality of life. Somehow we tend to believe that our situation is unique and therefore we don't speak up. And as a result, we try to handle life's difficulties on our own. Life does not give us unique situations. What you are going through many others before you have already faced or will come to face.

"When the walls close in, remember it's not the walls that will kill you. Ultimately, the silence does."

Many people isolate themselves and keep quiet. They somehow believe asking for help won't do any good. Just imagine someone sitting on his couch while his house is burning down and saying it won't make a difference if he shouts for help or not. Don't be fooled; silence isn't always golden. Here is an amazing thought – if you had no struggles in life, it would mean that you don't exist. Difficult moments are proof that you are alive. Be courageous and open up to someone. You will be amazed to find that there are people that care. Staying in hiding won't do you any good.

Be brave and bring your matters into the light. By telling someone it creates hope wherein silence there was none. Facing obstacles and challenges is part of humanity. When speaking up, you will discover that more people are facing similar situations. Connecting with others like you will create a sense of community. In communion there is unity and in unity, anything can be conquered. Isolation is one of the leading causes of death – it is what the lion does to its prey.

You will also discover revelation in unity, hope is born out of speaking up, and the seed of change will take root through exposure. Remember, as your victory draws closer the opposition will be at its most intense. It is at this very crucial point where you must push through because as you continue to do so, you'll experience a breakthrough.

Ultimately, we are not a product of our circumstances; we are a product of our response to those circumstances. So speak up and you will experience God move in unexplainable ways.

7. YOU

I don't know where you come from.
I don't know what you've done.
I don't know where you're hiding,
Or from what it is you run.
But what I do know is God has a
place for you in the sun.
You were shaped, molded, and designed.
You are truly one of a kind.
Even the Almighty looks at you,
and it blows his mind.
Forget about the past, it isn't you;
it's merely a product of you.
Stand up, walk tall, be brave, and have faith.
You're not simply here by chance,
but by God's intention.
Now go out and show the world,

His most prized invention.

8. SELF-BELIEF

I can do all things through Christ who strengthens me.

Philippians 4:13

Have you ever wondered why so many think so little of themselves? I believe that the root cause of this is that many have somehow traded in God's truth for the enemy's lie. This becomes a problem because our purpose is strongly linked to our self-belief. A lot of us discredit ourselves and our dreams because of our convictions. Think about how many times you wanted to do something and thought, "Can I really do this?" I wonder how many successful people would have killed their dreams because they stopped at, "can I really do this?" If you are your own worst enemy, then achieving your goals will be near impossible. If you cannot get past yourself, then you can forget about it. Rather than letting your thoughts sabotage you, treat them as your biggest asset and use them as a driving force to achieve your goals. Your goals require a lot of self-belief and self-love. Especially love because if you do not love yourself enough, you will unconsciously do things that will prevent you from achieving your goals.

Sometimes your self-belief is not only dependent on you. Many times in life, we need to draw from others. Many people will not believe in you, but the naysayers add no value to your life. Rather than focusing on them, you should shift your focus to the few who truly believe you can and trust in God, who knows you can. Don't believe what the masses say; just look at where they are today. They will say things like you can't or you won't because often it is what they say of themselves. Don't let their narrative interfere with yours. I have had many people give me funny looks when I told them I'm busy writing a book. Most people would laugh as if I just told them a joke. But I did not let it bother me, because I believe in myself, and I also knew that God thought it was a done deal. I wasn't going to publish a book to prove them wrong but to prove myself right. Imagine getting to the end of your life only to find out it was you stopping yourself all along.

> *"Self-belief starts when your questions*
> *turn into statements."*

So much of our self-doubt starts with us questioning ourselves. We ask ourselves questions such as "can I do this?" or "am I enough?" When in truth we'd be better of changing them into statements like "I can do this!" and "I am enough!" Jesus clearly says that you can do all things through Him, not some things, or just the things you believe you can do. Use words that are likely to build you up rather than breaking you down. This is an uncomfortable exercise for most because their inner conversation is of a different nature.

"You cannot consistently perform in a manner that is inconsistent with the way you see yourself."
Zig Ziglar

Self-belief will pave the way for what's possible, whereas self-doubt can't even lay a brick. Let your self-belief shape your reality and don't allow your reality to shape your beliefs. Ultimately, you'll meet the expectations of whatever you believe about yourself.

9. MADE-UP MIND

There's nothing as powerful as a made-up mind. Isn't it strange how two people can go through the same situation and have different experiences? Many of us have had so many past failures, and we use it as justification for our current circumstances. Phrases such as 'just as I thought' or 'just as I said' become our language and has a way of turning into 'just as I am'. Most people are more interested in proving themselves right than they are in living a better life.

For as he thinks in his heart, so is he.

Proverbs 23:7

Anyone who is looking for reasons not to change will find many. Most people point to past failures to justify their current state. Your past will always give you more than enough ammunition to stay the same. But your future also has ammunition of its own to bring forth change; it just depends on where your focus lies. A great future is built on the belief of what we can become. We must always be aware of our past but not be bound by it. Thoughts are responsible for so much of humanity's misery, but it can also be the catalyst for an abundant life.

Many people think that there's something wrong with them. Does their thinking cause their condition, or does the 'fact' that something is wrong with them cause them to think that way? Does the situation create the mindset, or is it the mindset that creates the situation? Allowing our minds to go unchecked is the cause of our biggest problems. Purposeful thoughts are what liberate us. Sadly for many, this is too much effort. You are not your past, focus on the future, and live the life you've always dreamed of!

10. THE WORST-CASE SCENARIO

"Your attitude towards something should not exist for the intent to change the fact. Its sole purpose is to change you."

We often fear the worst just because it is a possibility. There are always many given possibilities to any situation, but we somehow tend to believe the worst-case scenario to be the only one.

So many of us focus on that which poses the biggest threat to our future rather than focus on that which can bring us success. Just remember that the reality you create in your mind is the only one that counts. How many times have you feared the worst and then it came to pass?

For what I fear comes upon me, and what I dread befalls me.
Job 3:25

In Hebrews it tells us that faith is the substance of things hoped for, the evidence of things not seen. Remind yourself that there are always many possibilities, both good and bad. Let's shift our focus from what poses a threat to us and zoom in on that which can bring us success.

This is a struggle for many because they don't believe that they deserve success. Before you can achieve anything of worth, you must know that you are worthy. There are not near enough reasons for you not to be blessed.

God wants us to prosper and live the abundant life. But the worst-case scenario is in direct opposition to this. Ask yourself what value these scenarios add to your life? Do away with contemplating worst-case scenarios all they do is cripple you with fear.

11. A SHOT IN THE DARK

We must always take our chances even when the odds are stacked against us. Too often, when something seems impossible, we take one glance at it and never revisit the option. About a year ago I lost my memory stick in a shopping center. This memory stick was very important to me, as it had a lot of work on it – work that if lost, I would have to do all over again.

When I got home and realized that it was missing, I felt terrible. The first thing that crossed my mind was that I would never see it again. Coming to grips with this reality was not very pleasant. Despite feeling this way, another idea crossed my mind – why not take a shot in the dark? So I started retracing my steps and thought about all the shops I visited. In total, it was about three shops. Two of them were small, so I contacted them first, thinking it would be easier to spot. I phoned but no luck. The last shop I contacted was much bigger. I thought to myself, what are the odds? It reminded me of the movie *Dumb and Dumber* when Lloyd asks Mary what the chances are of her going out with him and she tells him the chances aren't good. He goes on to ask her, "not good as in one out of a hundred?" to which she replies, "More like one out of a million." He laughs and says, "So you're telling me there's a chance." It's funny, yet it teaches us a valuable lesson on how to approach obstacles and goals in life.

"The secret to success is taking a shot in the dark. It's not looking at your chances, but rather taking one."

You see, I had two choices; I could either phone the store or decide that it was not worth it. The worst that can happen is nothing. Never ask yourself what the chances are, rather believe that there is one. I drove there and asked them in person. And guess what? They found it… talk about a shot in the dark.

Sometimes a shot in the dark can hit something, and at the very least it's better than no shot at all because that is a guaranteed miss. And we'll never know if we don't try.

The following year I lost my wedding ring at a school camp, and again I thought, what are the odds of finding it? Once more, I took a shot in the dark and phoned them. A couple of weeks later and guess what – they found it! The difference between it being lost or found was a phone call, a shot in the dark. You might think your chances are one in a million, but you're also one in a million! You survived one out of forty million sperms. What are the odds of that happening? Yet, here you are! If there are things you want to attempt, and it looks unlikely, I suggest you take a shot in the dark. You just might find what you're looking for.

12. TRANSFORMATION

"If you want to change the facts, then start by facing them."

Consider how many things in your body, such as your kidneys, liver, and heart function automatically. However, you have full control over your mind – what you think about and what you don't. Therefore the mind is not something you want to leave unchecked because that's when unwanted thoughts can creep in. Once you take full ownership of your thinking, you will possess the power to change your life. We tend to live by the expectations others place on us, or sometimes those we place on ourselves. The problem is that they are often very low. If we truly want to transform, we need to live by the expectations God places on our lives. In the pursuit of transformation, there will be people that cannot envision it for you. Because so often they cannot envision their own lives changing for the better. Do not let their limiting beliefs limit you. The enemy will always remind you of your past because it's all he can see. God, however, places you in the present and gives you the promise of a better future.

Most people think they have their whole lives to

change, but too much time can be deceiving. Transformation is an intentional process. Do you know how many people desire to change but have no plan of action? They just cross their fingers and hope that things will get better. It is the same people who wish for their circumstances to change instead of changing their mindset towards their circumstances. Circumstances are ever-changing, but if you possess a consistently positive mindset, you'll be victorious over fluctuating circumstances, and it will make transformation possible.

Change is more likely to happen when you focus on that which you can change, and not on that which you can't. The past is one of the most significant change inhibitors known to man.

Saying "I want to" is not nearly as powerful as saying "I will". I used to say, "I want to write a book" but it was only when I started saying, "I will write a book" that unseen forces came to my aid. The most important and deciding factor for transformation in your life undoubtedly is God. When your car is broken down you take it to the mechanic. Likewise, if you desire transformation in your life, you should go to the one who made you – because with God all things are possible.

13. THE GIANT WILL FALL

All of us face so many challenges in life. And we tend to look at all our problems and get discouraged, leading us to an altogether sense of defeat and despair.

However, despite life's tragedies, we can be victorious. Maybe not today, but with persistence, in due time we will be triumphant. Ultimately it's your mindset that will make you victorious and not so much your actions. Your actions are but a by-product of your mind-set. Never underestimate the power of words, thoughts, and a positive attitude.

People tend to think a little positivity won't work! And as a result, it limits their growth. Growth is a necessary part of life and is vital to your future success. Why would you want to be any less than the person God created you to be? Always be careful of what you say about yourself it's more than just a statement it's a command.

A defeated mentality causes us to lose control and

power over our circumstances. But possessing a victorious mindset will enable us to overcome life's challenges. Consider David the little shepherd boy who challenged Goliath. David was fuelled with determination and faith in his creator. His main concern was not how he would defeat the Giant. He knew that it was something God had called him to do. And so his purpose was more important than any fears he might have had. Likewise, our focus must never be on the how but rather on the why.

So many people get stuck wondering how David was able to do it because that's the same question they ask of themselves, how? How will I overcome this? They get too caught up in how which often creates fear and leads them to do little or nothing about their situation.

Here's what I've learned – you might not know how to do it, but doing it wrong is far better than doing nothing at all.

Ultimately, it was not the stone that killed Goliath; it was David's faith that did. Without courage and faith, that little stone would have never even traveled through the air! Many times having giants in our lives is not the main problem, because we all have them. The biggest problem is that we don't have enough faith to face them.

So many things can prevent us from being victorious.

Excuses are one of the biggest culprits. And David knew that excuses would leave him defeated. I think David walked to the river and thought to himself "I'm not sure how I will do this, but the giant will fall", "I'm not sure how it will happen, but the giant will fall", "heck I have shortcomings, but the giant will fall", he instinctively knew that Goliath needed to fall and that it was his calling. He was the man that had to do it because if not him, then who? Some believe David took five stones to take out Goliath's four remaining relatives. Others believe David took five stones because even he knew that he was unlikely to hit him the first time trying, but whether it would take one try or five, he knew the giant would fall. There is no certain, guaranteed-to-work method.

But, what I can say without any fear of error is that staring at the giant will not make him fall. With a never-say-die attitude or a "does whatever it takes" mindset, you can defeat any giant in your life.

14. THE JOURNEY TO SUCCESS

"If you want to go all the way to the top, you must be willing to start at the bottom."

So many of us want to make it big, but we don't want to start small. We look at our role models and see where they are now, without giving as much as a thought to where they've been. We must remember the foundation of the mountain is much bigger than the summit. If we want to become like those we aspire to be, proximity is key. Because ultimately, who we hang out with has a direct impact on whom we become. Some of us have tried so many times. However, don't be too concerned about how many times you have to start over. If you have a clear goal and move in its general direction, you will get there eventually. We tend to focus on our shortcomings, rather on that which we have going for us. Begin to focus on what you can do, that will unlock the potential of doing that which you think you can't. It has been said that the easiest person to sidetrack is someone with no aim.

"Never give up on your dream because of the time it will take to accomplish it. The time will pass anyway."
Earl Nightingale

If we do not push ourselves as far as we can go, then how will we ever know what we are capable of? On this journey towards success, we must not mistake little progress for no progress. And your circumstances should never be a determining factor in reaching your goals. Consider this; the richest man in the poorest country is far richer than the poor in the richest country. There are many rooting for us and many others that would like to see us fail. This alone should give you motivation. On this journey, you will get pressure from all sides. But rather than it pushing you down, let it elevate you. Don't focus too much on results because that will only become visible at a later stage. The intent, however, can be seen immediately. And keeping this intent alive will allow you to keep going.

"You will either look back in life and say "I wish I had," or, 'I'm glad I did."
Zig Ziglar

Before you can reach the summit, you have to answer these four questions: where am I headed? How am I going to get there? Who do I need to assist me? And what must I leave behind? The road to success is a long and tough one. And the main reason most don't reach their destination is not that the road ends, but because their pursuit does.

15. JUST DO IT

In life, we are met with challenges that can overwhelm us. And what so often keeps us from getting stuck in, is that we focus on the obstacle and not our ability to overcome. To overcome any obstacle will take a lot of energy and effort. We must accept the fact that life will be difficult and there will be things we won't understand.

> *"Ask for help. Not because you are weak. But because you want to remain strong."*
>
> L. Brown

Your unwillingness to ask for help will be your unwillingness to grow. We need to get stuck in straight away and stay busy. Staying busy is vital! Becoming stagnant is what makes failures of us all. There will always be a million reasons why something won't work and probably much fewer reasons for why it will. But all you need is one reason, one good reason. One good reason is all the baby eagle needs to fly. One good reason is enough to put you into action.

*"Excuses are things you put on people and circumstances
that can't do a thing to change your situation."*

When I started writing this book, I didn't know what I was doing, and much less did I know the right steps to follow – I learned as I went. But I had a vision and the ability to get stuck in and just do it! And in doing, you must never forget your previous victories. Remind yourself that this time will be no different. Also, ask yourself how difficult can this be? And if someone did this before, why can't I? If it's not impossible, then there's always a chance it could be done. A possibility might not guarantee success, but believing it is impossible will guarantee failure. What are you waiting for? Get stuck in and just do it!

16. KEEP ON KEEPING ON

In life, people tend to knock on the first door, and when that door doesn't open, they give up. Perseverance is such a necessary component to make a success out of life. Many doors won't open – that's a fact. But one will open eventually; all we have to do is keep on moving and knocking until one opens.

> *"Winners do whatever it takes. Losers take whatever they can get."*

Losers rarely attempt anything in life because most of their battles are decidedly lost before they even start. I so vividly remember applying to do my postgraduate studies. My first attempt at applying failed miserably. Then I tried again somewhere else. This time I made more progress, but as always there were more hurdles to overcome. After many agonizing weeks, waiting in anticipation, they finally accepted me. Little did I know I was about to be confronted with another obstacle.

I was only allowed to study full time and not on a part-time basis. I wasn't prepared to leave my job at the time and sacrifice much-needed income. So there I was, back to square one. After two tries with two institutions, I had no luck. This was very discouraging and yet at the same time left me more determined than ever before. I so desperately wanted to be approved so that I could become an educator. And it is at this very crucial juncture people conclude that success was just not meant for them. It is also at this point where some people give up and is the reason so little succeed in life. It is here where we need to hang in there.

> *"Hanging on bridges the gap between the
> date people place on your goals, and the date
> God has set for it, to come to pass."*

I decided to not give up and go the extra mile. So I had another go, where another opportunity came my way. Here is what going the extra mile will do for you. It will be your bridge over troubled waters. That extra mile might just be the final one you need to get to your destination. Here I was applying yet again at yet another institution. I felt assured that this time I would hit the jackpot, but all I got hit with was yet another obstacle. The institution required a specific document from my previous qualifications, without which they would not allow me to apply. To make matters worse, the institution where I completed my sports studies did not have the information either, since I graduated about ten years prior. So I sent them the documents that I had in my possession, but it did not suffice. They simply refused, no matter how hard I pleaded. I had to dig deep into my archives quickly because the deadline was looming.

> *"Failure is an event, it's not a person."*
> Zig Ziglar

I kept on sending them documents in the hope that it would suffice. And just when I felt it was all over they suddenly approved me. And the rest, as they say, is history. I completed my post-graduate studies, and today I get to be a teacher.

Never give up, even when the odds are stacked against you. Maybe they are stacked against you for a reason? The bigger the dream, the bigger the odds against you will be. Just keep on keeping on, and someday something will give.

17. POINT OF VIEW

There was once a story told by an old lady sitting on her front porch. This story was about something that she had witnessed on a cold winter's afternoon, and that left her feeling very distressed. It involved a poor drunk homeless person that walked past her house, shouting profusely at someone further down the road. The lady decided to contact the police to sort the matter out. The police tracked down the man and started interrogating him. Their analysis of him was vastly different. They established that he was friendly, cooperative, and sober. He had a condition that made him walk staggered. And his clothes got tainted due to a scuffle caused by a criminal that robbed him. They had real sympathy for the helpless man. The "homeless person" described himself as being young at heart. He also said the chase gave him some much-needed exercise. He went on to say that this whole situation changed his life because, for the first time, he showed that he was brave enough to do something about a rather unfortunate situation.

"Your outlook on life changes, if you change what you look out for."

Here we have one situation with three different descriptions. What happens happens; but it is our point of view which ultimately changes the effect it has on our lives. Also, as in the case with the old lady, not knowing all we need to know gives us a limited vision. Your point of view greatly affects the impact any situation has on your life. Think about this for a moment – whatever it is that you can't see could be just the breakthrough you need.

A couch potato who loves the indoors does not give two hoots about traveling. But tell him he can never travel again for the rest of his life and suddenly he wants to go everywhere. Suddenly he has a new outlook on life. Yes, indeed, we don't know what we have until it's gone. And sadly most of us are gone before we knew what we had. Let that sink in for a while.

Becoming something great will require doing things that we don't like. However, we should never focus on how it makes us feel, but rather on what it can do for our lives and those around us. The main focus of the crucifixion for Jesus was not the pain it caused Him. Instead, His focus was on salvation for our lives. Always keep the main thing the main thing. And don't allow your circumstances to shape your point of view. Rather let your point of view shape your experiences in life. You can't change what has happened to you, but you can always change your outlook.

18. CONCLUSIONS

Isn't it strange how we are forever drawing conclusions about people, things, and circumstances in our lives? We make assumptions based on our own opinions. And opinions are like noses, everyone has one but unfortunately, they have holes in them.

"Nobody knows enough to be a pessimist."

W. Dyer

Remember what you consider to be trash the homeless person sees as treasure. What one person sees as dung, the other sees as compost. Your loose change is another man's fortune. The way you view things in your life is ultimately determined by your view of life. Using a positive outlook as a filter through which you perceive a situation in your life, will bring you joy. Someone might look at a problem, and that's all they see, while another looks at the same problem and sees the solution.

What you call the end of something God calls the beginning. What you call devastation today, God calls a miracle tomorrow. In the beginning, there was nothing, and God created the heavens and the earth. What you see as dirt, God uses to make a human being. So if you're looking at your life or an area of your life and it looks like rubbish, then remember God can use it to make things new.

There's a parable about a man who walked into a cage full of lions. He spent hours walking around, stroking them, and playing around. Many react and say that it is suicide. But little do they know the lions in the cage were just cubs. You'd say, but not all the details were given. But how many of us always ask for all the details? How many of us make conclusions in life without getting all the facts? So what else is in your mind? How many other things have you made conclusions about? What else have you boxed and buried? Be careful of the conclusions you make in life. Because making the wrong conclusions will undoubtedly end up adversely affecting your own life.

19. THE REALITY OF GOD

We are living in times where the reality of God seems to become less evident. For most people, God is dead to the world. They ponder the world around them and wonder if He even exists.

"The reality of God in your life depends on how much you focus on Him."

Many times we ask where God is amid what's going on in the world, or our lives. And it is at this very crucial juncture that people become estranged from Him. Then the reality of God becomes even less to where they can't experience Him at all. It is like God is dead. So many of us have unanswered questions about life that can so easily cause us to doubt God's existence. And when we operate out of doubt it is impossible to experience God. The way we experience Him is through faith. I have found in my life, and the experiences I've had, that the more I focus on Him, pray and spend time in the Word – the more He comes to the fore. If you consistently do that, you'll experience Him in even the most mundane things you do. God desires to have a relationship with you. He will always pursue you, but for God to become a reality in your life, you must keep your focus on Him. Even in the hard times... especially in the hard times.

"When you discover God is all you've ever needed, you'll realize He is all you've ever wanted."

Isn't it strange how people will have faith in electricity; something they can't see. But when it comes to God, they have no faith. They'll argue for the evidence of the electricity by pointing to the power it provides. But they forget that God's existence also provides power. This power is manifested in changed lives, healing, and many more miracles. But if you only see what you want to see, then that is all you will see. Every painting was made by a painter and likewise, creation was made by a creator.

We are all lost without God, without a savior, and left to our own devices we will perish. God has never moved an inch away from you. He also has a plan for your life and a vision that will blow your mind. We so often see ourselves as the world portrays us, but if we use their vision to achieve that which God has set out for us, we won't become the person He made us to be. The only way to live a life of significance is to see yourself as God sees you. So don't ask, "What will people think of me?", rather ask, "Who does God say I am?" God is knocking on your door, open up your heart, and invite Him in. Then make Him a priority and He will surely become a reality.

20. ABSOLUTE FAITH

*He replied, "You of little faith, why are you so
afraid?" Then he got up and rebuked the winds
and the waves, and it was completely calm.*

Matthew 8:26

Nothing calls upon your faith like having to overcome a seemingly impossible situation. However, faith isn't the only thing you need; you must also have no doubt. Many times we might have faith but a little bit of doubt will ultimately make us fail.

"Faith creates the ability to carry God's promises."

Unknown

Doubt is like a little hook but little though it is, it holds back the promise. Everything can come to nothing because of a grain of doubt. Yes, a grain of faith can also do the trick, provided there's no doubt involved. You cannot couple your faith with doubt and expect a miracle. Therefore, we must eliminate all doubt.

You must have total belief in yourself and your dreams.

Just remember if you have two opposite scenarios in your head, it can go either way! It can turn out good or bad. Try solely focusing on what you desire. People tend to feed their doubts much more than their faith because we tend to feed that which we practice the most.

> *"Your faith can move mountains. Your*
> *doubts can create them."*
>
> Martin Luther King Jr.

When disaster strikes, most people start to panic. Those whose faith is partnered with doubt, only kind of believe that things will get better. Too much doubt will cause you to focus on the how. Ladies and gentlemen, *how* is a faith killer. Dwelling on the how will cause you to lose faith. The *how* is Gods job, your job is to keep faith and trust in His promises.

The amount of faith you have is likely to increase the more you get to know God. Your doubts on the other hand can multiply the more you listen to the world. Endeavor to grow your faith so big that there's no room for doubt. It will be a constant battle. But to be successful and live an abundant life, we must have absolute faith.

21. THE ULTIMATE TIME THIEF

L ife will always hand us second chances – an opportunity to keep trying. You can right your wrongs; you can forgive, change, and live purposefully. All this takes time though, and time is the most valuable commodity on Earth. Time is limited and precious. And it makes matters worse when there's a thief that wants to steal it.

"Don't look for time; make provision for it."

People are constantly looking for time to do the things that matter in life. And yet so many fail in their attempts to get time. It's not that there isn't time... it's because they're not making time. We also waste time thinking about the past. And all the past really is, is lost time. We ponder about what was instead of what is to come. From today forth, you can go in a different direction to what you were going in yesterday. If you're on the wrong path and you change the direction slightly, you will end up in a completely different destination. So many people have this illusion that time is unlimited. But once we realize that it's not unlimited we will begin to treat it more kindly. The years you've spent in denial, defeat, anger, and bitterness might be over, but so is the time and you will never get it back.

I can never relive my school years, or redo the harmful words I said to a loved one. I am not pointing it out to make you depressed. I merely want to show you how the enemy robs you of life's most precious gift called time. He steals your joy by causing you to react to life's circumstances instead of responding to them. He takes your focus away from what matters to that which doesn't. If the enemy can achieve this, then he can also steal your time. All he wants to do is take you away from the present moment – and that is all we will ever have. It is in the present where we find God, the giver of time.

Therefore, we need to be careful with what we spend our time on because time will run out. And depending on where you've invested your time, it can either be sand through the hourglass, or seeds in the garden. The best possible time for change to take effect is now. Reclaim your life, be what you've always wanted to be and do what you've always wanted to do. Time is something we only have a limited amount of. Don't be fooled into thinking you have forever. Be careful of the ultimate time thief! He's waiting for you when you wake up.

22. SIX FEET UNDER: THE BERNIE STORY

In my early days, I started speaking at a non-profit organization that assists people who live on the streets of Cape Town. It is here where I met a fascinating character by the name of Bernie. He had it all, a good job, a house, a wife, and children. But unfortunately, he also had a drinking problem which ultimately cost him all that was dear to him in life. And so it landed him on the streets.

Amid his troubles, he was a huge inspiration to me. One day he was traveling and after a long haul decided to take an overnight pit stop at a gas station. And there just so happened to be a bar around the corner. So Bernie thought he'd have a couple of cold ones before he goes to sleep. Unfortunately, a couple became a couple too many. The next day Bernie woke up under a tree, with a hangover and in no-man's-land. He felt his pockets, and everything was gone! His cell phone, wallet, driver's license... everything. He said that he felt like they robbed him of his identity – and suddenly he felt like he was nobody. He was lost, literally and figuratively.

In this state of depression and utter disbelief, a voice came to him saying "Bernie look around you, look where you are". And as he looked up, he saw that he was in a graveyard. He had no clue how he ended up in a graveyard of all places. The voice went on to say, "Look at the dates on the gravestones". He looked, and it read 1892, 1956, 2011, 1989, and so on. The voice continued, "Bernie, these people are all six feet under the ground, but your feet are still firmly on the ground. That means you are alive, and that today you have an opportunity to right your wrongs. You can forgive, love more, and be who I made you to be."

What a revelation, and how true. Remember this when you pass by a graveyard again. And remind yourself that you're still alive. Your feet, no matter what you've done, are still firmly on the ground.

23. THE INTERVIEW

When being interviewed for a job, the number one question you'll get asked is, "Where do you see yourself in five or ten years?" The answer you give could be the difference between being hired or not. I always used to ask myself why they would ask such a question. Why do so many companies ask that specific question? After giving it some careful consideration, I came to a conclusion.

"See yourself somewhere, or end up nowhere."

Here's the thing, if you don't see yourself somewhere in five years from now, you're likely to end up where you don't want to be. Companies want goal-orientated people, and if you can't see yourself in a specific place in five years, you are less likely to take them to the place they have in mind. It's like those pictures we used to draw as children, called connect-the-dots. Where is your next dot? Most people don't even know where they are headed next.

A person who sees themselves in a specific place in the future will make specific moves to get there. They use their time wisely and operate with a sense of urgency. If you don't have a clear picture in your mind of where you want to end up, life and its circumstances will decide for you. You'll end up somewhere guaranteed. So either you decide or life, the people in it and its circumstances will.

Someone with a clear vision has a clear path and decides with clarity. They do not get distracted by secondary activities. An unclear vision equals an unclear path. If you get into your car and just drive with no destination in mind, you'll be forever driving. The Bible says that a man without a vision dies. This shows us how important having a vision really is. You must always endeavor to form a clear vision in your mind of your future. Where do you see yourself? Hold on to that vision and work towards it like your life depends on it. Why? Because it does. Before God made you, He envisioned you and then he formed you in your mother's womb. So, where do you see yourself five years from now?

24. THE BIG DEBATE

Arguments are daily occurrences. No matter whom you are or where you go, you'll encounter them. And finding middle ground seems to be an endless struggle.

People will die for their beliefs and viewpoints, regardless of it being true or not. It's true to them. So many people associate their opinions with who they are. So when someone comes along and opposes their opinions, they perceive it as if they are being opposed. This couldn't be further from the truth.

*"Before you can say that you're right. You first
have to ask yourself if you might be wrong."*

Arguments seldom start based on fact versus fiction. The problem is that people believe they are right regardless of the truth. They believe their viewpoint is the only truth because it is all they're looking at. People will sacrifice growth at the expense of a small victory. Most of the arguments we have are so trivial. We usually get caught up in senseless arguments and as a result forfeit our peace for a bit of satisfaction.

Lack of knowledge also plays a big role in the origin of arguments. People are not willing to acknowledge other viewpoints because then they believe theirs has no merit. This is not the case; it merely means you have an opportunity to learn something new. A sense of insecurity also plays a significant role. When people think little of themselves, they will fight tooth and nail for their beliefs. Because they think their value is found in what they believe in. When in reality it's found in who you are. So what if people don't agree with you, it does not that change your beliefs or theirs?

"At the end of every clash with your fellow man, ask yourself… did the Devil win? Or was God triumphant?"

Many years ago, I heard an example of an argument illustrated by a card between two parties. One side of the card is blue and the other side red. When both parties are forever arguing without coming around to the other's side, all they'll ever see is blue… or red.

Many arguments have truths in them… on both sides! Mostly both parties have a leg to stand on. Popular belief says one is right, and one is wrong when, in reality, many arguments could hold merit on both sides. Emotions can so easily cloud our judgment. Choose your battles wisely they so often take more than what they give. Giving the matter some careful consideration in time will allow you to assess the matter on its merit.

Leaving it unattended can cause unnecessary bitterness and pain.

*"An apology carries more weight if it
changes your approach"*

Most people are unwilling to forgive others. Not because of what others did but because it was done to them! Take the focus away from you and humble yourself, then the forgiveness can take its full effect. The Bible tells us to die to ourselves. If you can make this practice a number one priority, it will become very hard for you to get caught up in an argument. Most arguments aren't worth the fight. Engage in a senseless argument, and you might "win", but in the grand scheme of things, you'll lose.

25. TEAM EFFORT

If you are anything like me, then somewhere in your life you've asked God to come through for you – to answer a prayer, open a door, or to perform a miracle. God still performs miracles. And I believe God can perform many more, but I also believe that we have a part to play.

> *"The good Lord is Almighty, but He appreciates a helping hand."*
>
> Unknown

And so by doing what we can do, I believe God will do what we can't. It is said that God helps those that help themselves. If we want God to come through for us, then we must play our part as well. If you're willing to do what God requires of you and put things in motion, then I believe God has the power to finish it. Some say that the only will stronger than that of God is your own. I've heard so many people say that God has a plan for their lives. And then I see them sitting on the proverbial couch. Legs crossed, hands folded, and eyes gazed to the heavens. Stagnantly praying and hoping that someday and somehow God will come through for them.

I hate to be the bearer of bad news, but it's unlikely to happen for you if that's your approach. God had a plan for David's life. God made a giant fall, but David had to swing the stone. God split the Red Sea, but Moses kept the faith. We sometimes ask so much of God and then expect to do so little. I believe the emphasis must be on you and God working together. Ultimately, God will get all the glory, but for a miracle to take place, it needs to be a team effort.

God has a purpose for your life, all He requires of you is to sow the seed, and He will grow the tree.

"Success will happen for you when you primarily focus on the why and not the how"

Always make sure you have a big enough reason to go after your dreams. Too many forget their motivation and focus too much on how it will come to pass. Many people do not pursue greatness, not because they don't want to, but because they are content. They trade their happiness for contentment. If you prioritize contentment over your happiness, then all you will ever be is content. Creating a better life requires you to step out of your comfort zone. Because it is when you step out of your comfort zone where miracles can happen. If your self-belief can match that of God's belief in you, then anything and everything is possible.

People so often say they want to be successful, but they're not willing to do what it takes to become successful. They want health, but they're not willing to exercise, they want to save money, but they don't want to stop spending. Make no mistake there's always a price to pay. How deep are you willing to dig in your pockets to pay the price? God has a purpose for your life, but don't leave it to chance, get up, act, and then I believe He will perform the miracle.

26. FOCUS

Focus is so often an underestimated aspect when it comes to our success in life. What we focus on will play such a vital role in making a success out of our lives. Consider the effect of the sun through a magnifying glass. If the glass is held still it can start a fire. But when moved around, no matter how powerful the sun, nothing will happen. Likewise, if our focus is forever shifting then nothing is likely to happen for us.

The Bible tells us to keep our eye single; to keep our focus on the job at hand. Countless things in life can steal our focus. So we need to intentionally concentrate if we want to fulfil our purpose on Earth.

"Keep your focus on the promise, and not on the problem."

We are faced with so many difficulties and challenges in our lives. They will always exist, but concentrating on them will only cause us to lose focus. As sure as there are problems in life there is also a promise that awaits us. God has a promise for our lives, but if we lose the focus of this promise, we will not receive it.

"It's not what you look at that matters, it's what you see."

Henry David Thoreau

We have many positives and negatives in our daily lives, but the positives do not diminish because of the negatives. It only diminishes when we focus on the negative. Let's also not lose focus on the fact that our time on Earth is but a small part of our eternal journey. Many people are left paralyzed by what happens to them on Earth. But by keeping your focus on things above will place your life into perspective. In life, you can lose many things, but whatever you do, don't lose your focus.

27. IDENTITY

Have you ever looked at your id photo and thought is that really me? Do you know who you truly are? So many of us go through life being someone we were never intended to be. Some of us might get as far as to throw away the old self. But if you don't have a revelation of whom you were created to be, then you'll remain who you are. Imagine an addict who finally decides to quit, but then relapses because he doesn't know his true identity. In such a case, someone will likely revert to their old ways.

Every day is an opportunity to change. Not into whom you want to be, but who God made you to be. You were not born a certain way; you are not the product of your DNA. You are the way you are because you choose to be. It is difficult for a soccer player to become a swimmer. Not because of the transition but because of the lack of vision. It's not because he can't become a swimmer, it's because he can't see himself as one. He is a soccer player because that is what he were yesterday and the day before that. Our choices over time form a mould which we assume is our identity.

"In a world full of opinions, the one that will ultimately shape you will be the one you pay the most attention to."

Some people continue to act in a certain way because of what the world tells them. They persist to play the role, silently unaware of their true identity. If you don't know your true identity, you will never become who God created you to be. Just because you did something a certain way for years, does not mean it is you. You are not what you do! A cat who acts like a lion is not a lion; he remains a cat. I believe that every person is inherently good. It's adopting the wrong identity that corrupts them.

We listen to what the world says instead of what God says. After a while, so many of us begin to accept who we have become. A false identity that says you're a loser, failure, addict, or perhaps just another human being. And when you resign yourself to being nobody, you'll start to live like one and get set in your ways.

*"The difference between a groove and
the grave is only the depth."*

Unknown

As humans, we are very quick to compare ourselves to others, and comparison tends to make us feel inadequate. The only person you must ever compare yourself to is the person God created you to be. If you can do that then God will place you in positions you didn't even apply for.

> *"If you want to know what you're made of,*
> *then just look at who made you."*

The definition of acceptance is to believe something to be valid or correct. Don't ever allow yourself to accept who you are at the expense of what you can become. Because if you put yourself in such a position, then you're in a situation where you are unlikely to change. Of course, this is not an issue if you're living out your true identity. God made you in His image. That should give you some indication of how valuable you are. Don't choose an identity based on what you did, or who you were yesterday. Assume your true identity on the back of what God says about you.

28. WORTHY

How do you see yourself? How valuable do you think you are? These are such important questions that I believe everybody should ask themselves. Because if you think you aren't worth much, you will think that what you do isn't worth much either. Inferiority prevents people from doing great things.

If only you can comprehend how valuable you are, you'll achieve a level of success that matches that worth. There has never been anyone like you, nor will there ever be! Feeling like you're not worth much brings about a state wherein you contribute little. A horse without its legs can't compete in a race. But a horse with legs that believes it can't run is far worse! We are all human beings with equal worth, and our value doesn't increase or decrease by what we do or don't do. Our worth is found in who made us.

"You are a masterpiece because the Master made you."

Stop concentrating on what others think of you and remind yourself of what God says about you. Remember, if you go through life with a 'poor old me' attitude, others are likely to treat you accordingly. You are a unique individual with unique talents. And when you discover your true worth, you have the potential to change the world.

29. ONE DAY

You've probably heard people say 'one day' so many times. One day I will do this, and one day I'll achieve that. Of course, it's great to have goals but the problem with 'one day' is, if you're not careful, it'll pass you by. One day has a significant element of delay and procrastination associated with it. If your goals are important to you, then you will start working on it today. One day is far too vague.

"If you don't start today, your one day is but an illusion."

I have seen many a calendar, and it has many dates on, but nowhere does it say 'one day'. Most people think they have forever to achieve their goals. Therefore, someday somewhere in the future does not bother them. They are under the illusion they have their whole life to achieve it. 'One day' will cause you to get stuck in secondary activities and put your dreams on hold.

Your 'one day' hinges on your every day. The people that make it in life cannot pinpoint a single day. Because they have so many days to point to, and this ultimately brought them to where they are in life. A 100-meter athlete wins the gold medal in under 10 seconds, yet it is ten years of hard work that makes it possible. And if you want to make your dreams a reality then I suggest you throw away someday and start today.

30. WISHING AND WANTING

There is a distinct difference between wanting to change and only wishing to do so. I spent a long time aspiring to change but it was only ever a wish. I would drink and smoke myself into oblivion on a Saturday, and on Sunday morning I'd regret it. Then I'd inspect myself in the mirror, and utter the following words, "I want to change". However the next weekend would come along and I'd do it all over again. This cycle would repeat itself over and over. It's an exhausting process – trying to be the person God wants you to be while still doing your own thing.

In reality, I never wanted to change; I only wished to. Wanting and wishing are two entirely different things. Ultimately your actions will show that you're serious about changing, not your words! If your desire to change is but a wish, then you'll stay the same. You see, wanting is an action, wanting is doing! Wanting is an investment, an oath, a dedication, and a covenant. If you say you want to change, yet you aren't doing anything about it, then all you're doing is wishing.

*"Maturity is not the product of time. It's
the product of revelation."*

True change starts when you act. It's no good pondering over that which you don't want to be. Instead, use that energy to focus on who you want to become.

Finally, and most importantly, you'll never change if you can't envision yourself a changed man. Envision the person God wants you to be, and then work towards it with urgency. Don't lose that picture in your mind, hold on to that vision with everything you have. As long as you see yourself as the old self, no amount of effort will bring about a permanent change. Remember, if you cannot see, you cannot be! Don't be fooled wishes are only found in fairytales. But a strong desire, clear vision, and the help of God Almighty will bring about change in you.

31. THE MIND OF CHRIST

For who has understood the mind of the Lord so as to instruct him?" But we have the mind of Christ.

1 Corinthians 2:16

Many years ago, I gave my life to Christ. But after that day, there have been many times where it almost felt like I've taken it back. This was a rather unpleasant back-and-forth scenario. Words cannot express how important giving your life to Christ is. But if you don't give your mind too, you're fighting an uphill battle. So what does it mean to give your mind to Christ? Firstly and most importantly I believe it means being mindful of Him. Being conscious of who Christ is and what he has done for you. If you can give your undivided attention to the word daily, then it will allow you to have victory on Earth and not only when you get to heaven. It's easy for the enemy to pounce if you don't give your mind to Christ. The Devil is okay with you giving your life to Christ as long as you keep your old way of thinking. The enemy knows this creates an opportunity for you to slip back into your old ways. The Devil's chief interest is your mind. And that is exactly where he takes you on.

The Bible says as a man thinks, so is he. Someone that swims in the sewers all day won't come out smelling like roses. Likewise, you cannot think negatively all day and expect to live victoriously. Our desire must be to have the mind of Christ. A life dedicated to Christ is not based on just one moment; it's an ongoing commitment. If you allow yourself to drop your guard the Devil will seize your mind. The enemy of our souls never sleeps and neither should you.

The day you decide on being intentional about your thought life is the day you'll start to be victorious. This will also lay a foundation for God to rewire your brain, not for a week, not for a month but for good! If you stop steering your thoughts the enemy will take the wheel.

I've heard many people say that this "God thing" doesn't work for them, which proves it's all about what they can get out of it. And that's not what Christianity is all about. No matter how far gone you are, or how deep you're in, you can always change by changing your thoughts. Listen to that voice in the back of your head that whispers "turn around". I once saw a shirt that read, "Every second is a chance to turn your life around". The process of change is a never-ending one, but it can start to change the very second you decide to. The very second you decide to think like Christ, matters not only can change, but will change. Your mind and your thoughts hold the key to a victorious life. So give your mind to Christ, and He will transform you.

32. A NEW CREATION

*Therefore, if anyone is in Christ, the new creation
has come: The old has gone, the new is here!*

2 Corinthians 5:17

So many people believe they are incapable of changing. They mostly feel this way because of the things they've done. Those deeds make them feel unworthy of change. Consider Paul from the Bible, a mass murderer of Christians, having such a mindset. Paul knew that our salvation doesn't depend on what we do or don't do; it's confirmed in what Christ has already done for us.

*But Jesus told him, "Anyone who puts a hand to the plow
and then looks back is not fit for the Kingdom of God."*

Luke 9:62

Make no mistake, to sin, is wrong, but nothing is so bad that it cannot be forgiven. Once you truly believe God forgives your sins, your belief will set you free. It is also your belief that will carry in it the seed of the new you. Change can happen if you believe God forgives, but if you think your past deeds outweigh your ability to change you will continue to be your old self. You'll forever continue to be something you don't want to be because you're in a jail which reminds you of what you've done. And that what you've done is unforgivable.

God did not come to make you a better person; he came to make you a new creation. You must never dwell on what you've done, but rather on what you can do from here on out. Dwelling on the past holds no power for you to change your life, yet that is what most people focus on. Too much focus on the past will take away the present moment and steal our future.

> *"A seed which believes it's only a seed*
> *will never become a tree."*

Nothing can keep you from God's grace. And nothing can stop you from changing except your mindset. You can't change while still complaining about your current state! If a seed did that, it would die. A seed grows to become what it ought to be and doesn't give a thought about what it is. Anyone can become a new creation if Paul could, so can you. Remember, your sin doesn't define you. Your definition lies in who God made you to be. Paul knew that his sins would have consequences. But he also knew that he was forgiven. Accepting God's forgiveness and grace enabled him to change. And it also allowed him to set his eyes firmly toward the future. Paul went on to write many books in the Bible and became one of the biggest role players in God's Kingdom. Paul had no excuses, and neither do you.

"Transformation occurs when you see yourself as God sees you."

If we don't believe in God's word, then by default we accept to stay the same. Ultimately it is not life and its circumstances that shape us, it is our beliefs. You can change by accepting God's truth, or you can listen to the enemy's lies, and stay the same. After today, you don't ever have to be the same person again, except if you choose to be.

33. THE MASTER'S PLAN

He will wipe every tear from their eyes. There will
be no more death' or mourning or crying or pain,
for the old order of things has passed away.

Revelation 21:4

Just imagine there being no creator, and therefore no creation, no universe, and ultimately no you. And since there is a huge void of absolute nothingness, it means there is no hurt, pain or challenges of any kind. Good as the latter sounds it would also mean no joy, no gift of life, no God, and ultimately no eternal life. This is a very scary thought to wrap your head around. However, it allows us to put life and its challenges into perspective.

If presented with the following options, either a big void or creation which one would you choose? You would naturally choose the latter without giving it any thought. Because in your life, even with all its difficulties and challenges gives you heaven to look forward to. We so often wonder why there's suffering in the world or why we experience pain in our lives. But here is an even more painful thought –no existence, no life, and no God. That is probably the scariest conceivable thought anyone could have. Creation shows us how blessed and lucky we are to be alive, and that we have a God who loves us. We must make the most of our lives so that what we do will echo in eternity.

*"Gratitude does not only make you hold on
to what you have. Gratitude also shows you
what's important to hold on to."*

Even if you don't believe in God, your existence is still not of your own doing. Therefore, we must be grateful for the life we've been given, and keep the faith, even amid some tragic experiences, that the grandmaster is weaving everything together to create a tapestry. A tapestry we cannot see right now. But will one day no doubt all make sense.

34. THE TRUTH SHALL SET YOU FREE

Then you will know the truth, and the
truth will set you free.

John 8:32

The truth plays such a vital role in shaping the outcome of our lives. With this in mind, I believe we have to answer some very important questions. What thoughts and beliefs are dominating your mind, and what do you believe to be the absolute truth? The answers you give to these questions will no doubt have a big impact on your life. This becomes an important issue when we consider how many people are living a life based on lies. Lies such as believing Bible verses are only words. Yet unknowingly these people's lives are governed by words. Words are not just words, but conceived thoughts.

For many years I believed in things that weren't true because I did not seriously question those beliefs. And when we don't question lies, they become a way of life. The adage, "if I knew better I'd do better" still rings true. Sometimes we can't conceive a better life because of what we don't know. Imagine a bird who doesn't know his wings can make him fly. What a tragic existence indeed. Most of us have been taught that what we don't know won't hurt us. When in reality, some of what we don't know will hurt us. Ignorance is not bliss!

Deceit and lies will always occupy a space. Just make sure that space isn't between your ears. The reason many people don't believe in themselves is that often the lie is easier to believe than the truth. The lie that says you can't do any good because you're no good. Again the adage, "truth is stranger than fiction" rings true. However, just because that might be the case doesn't make the truth anything less than it is. So many people believe in senseless lies, and at the same time, they discard miracles as being stuff you only find in fairytales.

As humans, we tend to discard that which we cannot understand to be a lie. If I were to explain to you the finer nuances of how exactly a microwave works you'd be in disbelief, but yet it warms your food. In the same way, we might not always know how God operates, but the end result will meet our needs. The enemy makes several attempts to entrench a lie as part of your mindset, and if left unattended, it becomes accepted as the truth. Challenge your beliefs in pursuit of the truth. And then the truth shall surely set you free!

35. THE BATTLE

Fight the good fight of the faith. Take hold of the eternal life to which you were called when you made your good confession in the presence of many witnesses.

1 Timothy 6:12

Life on earth can be described as one big battle, a battle that so often gets the better of us. So many things in life will try to derail us and take us off the path that was meant for us. And if we're not willing to fight we will surely lose the battle.

"Life is a fight for territory and once you stop fighting for what you want, what you don't want will automatically take over."

Les Brown

In the grasslands of Africa, the lion waits for the season of rain to end. This is the lion's perfect opportunity to be successful in catching its prey. The lion instinctively knows that the season of rain means prosperity for its prey. It is a time when its prey is well-nourished and hydrated. And as a result, can flourish in its environment. However, the lion also knows the season of famine, and drought is coming. And when that season begins then life for its prey becomes very hard. Resources are low, and fatigue sets in. It is then that the lion grabs his opportunity to strike. Likewise, the enemy of our souls is waiting for a season in our life when tragedy strikes.

The thief comes only to steal and kill and destroy; I have come that they may have life and have it to the full.

John 10:10

Have you ever felt as though someone has stolen something from you? Like something is missing in your life? The Devil's number one priority is to take from you and ultimately destroy you. However, God's aim is to give you life in abundance. We must be aware of both these realities. The enemy entices us by drawing a line. And once you cross that line, he'll draw another one. The more lines you cross, the further away he knows you are from God. And the further away you are from God, the more he can manipulate you.

"The only thing the Devil needs to defeat you is your permission."

So many of us lose life's battles because we fail to recognize we're in one. There is a story about a man lying on his deathbed. He was afraid of dying as the doctors gave him a limited prognosis. So he asked his wife if she thought he would survive. She replied by asking him if he wants to live? And he answered with a resounding yes. His wife then told him, "Well, in that case, I suggest you hold on to God's hand and fight as you've never fought before." Her husband replied by asking, "What if I fight and end up dying anyway?" His wife then answered saying, "Then we will know that it was God's plan, but if you don't fight, we will never know!" Likewise, in life, if you're not willing to fight, the world will never know what you are made of... or what you were made for!

36. THE PICTURE

Have you ever been to an art exhibition, looked at a particular painting, and thought "what on earth was the artist thinking?" People have an inherent need to know why and how things happen. And because many have a negative mindset, they tend to fear the worst. Remember the only reality that counts, is the one you form in your mind.

Isn't it funny how we make up our minds? We are so quick to link uncertain times that lie ahead in our life, with times that look terrible. We adopt a narrative that says our best days are behind us, when the Bible clearly tells us that our best days are still ahead. God has many blessings in store for your life. The future might be unknown, but we serve an all-knowing God.

Whether you believe it or not... you have a picture in your mind. And it can either be dark and grim or bright and beautiful. We form the latter out of always looking for the good in each situation, and the former out of always thinking the worst. Yes, the future is unknown, and we do not know what will happen. But we can choose to paint a picture out of expecting the best or the worst. If you expect the best, and the worst happens, you can still live a life of victory. On the flip side, if you expect the worst and the best came to pass, then your circumstances might change, but you won't.

Ultimately, we are defined by the picture we have in our minds. A bright picture will enable us to deal with life positively. A mind that forms a bright picture will be able to draw from it in difficult times. While a dark picture will end up drawing from us. We are not defined by what happens to us, but rather by whom we were through it all.

In the times we are living in, forming a positive picture is no doubt a struggle. But if we stop struggling, we will lose the picture. And if we lose that picture we can also lose ourselves in the process. Decide today to paint a bright picture that will allow you to rise above any circumstance you'll ever face. This will enable you to live a life of victory in a dark and fallen world.

37. THE HUMAN CONDITION

The heart is deceitful above all things, and desperately wicked: who can know it?

Jeremiah 17:9

So much of what we do and the way we do it are because of our conditioning. Meaning it's the way we've trained our mind, body, thoughts, and habits. This conditioning brings about a day to day living that gets fortified by repetition. Every day, we unknowingly program ourselves by what we feed our minds with. And over time this programming then ends up programming us.

Ultimately we get to choose the program that governs our life. After many years of programming yourself it becomes like a set of laws that subconsciously dictates the way you live your life. Train your dog to attack, and after a while, he'll do so without being told. Likewise, if you train your mind to think negatively it'll produce negative results without any effort. When you were young and had to start brushing your teeth, it took many deliberate decisions to form the habit. Now you do it automatically without giving it a thought. You don't decide to do it anymore; your programming decides for you.

We often do things that we know are wrong and yet as we approach doing it, we find ourselves to have to fight off the urge. Fighting the thought and battling the mind. And so often we succumb to these temptations. And so we might have good intentions but if we possess the wrong mindset then our efforts will be futile.

Years of wrong thinking have conditioned your mind and from there your heart. Your conditioning can either fortify the person God made you be or destroy it. Therefore, we must endeavor to recondition the mind, no matter the cost.

"I have trained my mind, and my body will follow."

Unknown

Whatever beliefs you have always ask yourself this question – is it a fact or a thought? Your beliefs aren't always facts; nevertheless you will live out what you believe in. And if you believe the enemy's lies, you are allowing the enemy to shape you.

We are so prone to think all our best efforts are in vain. Yet God is always working behind the scenes. Allow God's words to program you and He will make inroads

– just don't give up. God has changed me in ways I never thought possible. Everything we do, say or think affects change in us no matter how small. Remember that every man's demise came about because of a series of small acts done repeatedly. Similarly, every man's victory also came about due to a series of small tasks done repeatedly. The sum of your thoughts will undoubtedly have a result. And depending on what you fill your mind with; it will either be a good or bad result.

Repeated negative thoughts have the potential to corrupt you. Avoid spending time with negative people, because eventually, you will adopt their way of thinking. Always take responsibility for your own thoughts; this will give you full control over your mind. Small steps of progress over time will bring about a monumental shift in you. Consider that tornadoes start with a light breeze, and termites destroy a house with several small bites. Likewise, you can start to reprogram your mind and little by little change the condition you're in.

38. DREAMS

For a dream comes with much business, and
a fool's voice with many words.

Ecclesiastes 5:3

We all have dreams, even if it was just once upon a time. But, as we grow older, and the reality of life kicks in, our dreams can fade and die. This can be because we've encountered so many failures. And therefore we believe that we're not worthy of any success and that dreams are for a select few only. After all, why do so few become successful? Therefore, we give up on our hopes and dreams. This happens because we look at our dreams through the lens of our experiences and what others have said about us. And the more we look through those lenses, the more our dreams fade and die. That's why a good deal of people gives up on their dreams.

"If all you've experienced is failure. Just remember,
It is where you are… and not who you are"

We somehow mistake our failures for who we are. You are not what you've done; you are who God made you to be. If only you could see yourself through the lens God sees you then those dreams you've buried will resurrect.

"If you want God to use you in a powerful way, then just start by putting up your hand."

When God made you; He also had a vision for your life. He did not just create you; He created you for a purpose! What's the point of any creation if it doesn't have a purpose? What's the purpose of a car if it can't take you anywhere? What's the purpose of a toaster if it can't toast your bread? The answers are obvious, yet somehow when it comes to God's most important creation; we believe the same rule does not apply. So many believe that with seven billion people on Earth, there can only be a select few who can achieve their dreams. This is because people believe there are only a select few dreams on offer. This couldn't be further from the truth. My dream was to write a book, and if I believed there could only be x amount of authors on Earth, you would not have the privilege of reading this book.

What changed my perspective is something I heard someone say. And this is that every person has a dream and a purpose, and nobody can get your dream because it was given to you! And if you don't achieve the dream, it's not because someone else took it but because you didn't take it. Many authors can write their books, but they can't write the one that was meant for you. Many musicians can sing their songs, but they can't sing yours. Artists can create pieces of art, but they can't make your masterpiece.

Once we realize that our dream and purpose will always be there regardless of whether we achieve it or not. Then it will allow our dreams to be seized because we know that nobody can take our stuff. Once you realize that all that's standing between you and your dreams is yourself, you will start working towards it with urgency.

> *"Your dreams can not be taken away or destroyed.
> It can only be achieved... or not be achieved."*

We must also not be fooled into thinking that just because we all have a dream that somehow we will automatically achieve it, or that it will happen by chance. Our dreams do not become a reality just because it exists. It becomes a reality when we have continued belief in that dream and work towards it.

> *"If you want to make a difference in the world, then
> you're never going to do it from your comfort zone."*
>
> A. Kitching

Your dreams will not be found in your comfort zone, it requires you to step out and take the leap of faith. There are plenty of people who don't go after their dreams because of excuses, of which there will always be an unlimited supply. The world will always try to wake you up from your dream state, but you must resist this at all times. Just keep your eyes closed, keep dreaming, and never wake up from the purpose God has called you for!

39. THE VISION

"Vision is the art of seeing what is invisible to others."

Jonathan swift

A clear vision plays such a vital role in making a success out of life. I used to be in a never-ending cycle. On weekends I would indulge in alcoholic beverages and smoke the odd cigarette. At times I would get so intoxicated that I could not remember what happened the day before. Besides physically feeling horrible the next day; mentally and spiritually, I would also feel lost.

The day after, which was usually a Sunday, I'd have a very empty feeling. So I decided to try harder next time around. Try harder not to engage in these activities and yet still have a good time. And so the next weekend would come, and true as Bob, I'd slack off a bit. But the next day I would still have a hangover although this time not as bad. Yet I still felt empty inside, so I decided to switch to non-alcoholic drinks and no cigarettes. I simply had to try harder, and dig a little deeper.

"No matter how hard you try to better yourself. Your success thereof will largely depend on the way you see yourself. The vision will always far outweigh the effort."

The next weekend came along, and although somewhat of a struggle, I'd be successful. And so with that effort, I'd feel like I had overcome my bad habit. But the victory was short-lived. Because on the very next occasion I would drink myself into another religion and wake up on a Sunday morning feeling very despondent. All my efforts for nothing! And so I told myself the next time I'll just try harder. Maybe I was doing something wrong. It felt like all I had left was a prayer.

"You told everybody I don't have a chance. You told 'em I don't have nothing but a prayer. Chump, all I need is a prayer because if that prayer reaches the right man, not only will George Foreman fall, mountains will fall!"

Muhammad Ali

God gave me a revelation that changed my life forever, a new perspective to get this elusive monkey off my back for good. He showed me that no matter how hard I'd try if I kept on seeing myself as a drunken party animal, I would always fall back to the default vision I had of myself. You can change but only if you change the way you see yourself. So how can you change the way you see yourself? By looking at what God says about you. Then out of that form a new vision of you and constantly re-enforce it by staying in the word. Envisioning yourself as this new person every day will bring about a transformation in your life!

40. NEVER SETTLE

So many people get to a stage in their lives where they don't believe things can change for them. And if you're not careful this ongoing belief will fortify the current state you're in. It is a belief that says this is how life will always be and that somehow it was meant to be this way.

"It's not the current situation of things not changing in your life that seals your fate. It is your belief things will never change that ultimately seals it."

There once was a story about a guy who was stuck in a hole for a very long time. In the beginning, he tries to climb out, but all his efforts are futile. The more he tries, the less he seems to get anywhere. During this whole process, little bits of sand and gravel fall to the bottom of the pit. After an endless struggle, he finally decides to quit. Sadly, he did not realize that the more he tried, the more sand and gravel will fall to the bottom of the hole. This would have caused the hole to fill up and thus enable him to elevate himself out of there.

It's never our ability that stops us; it is our mentality.

That poor man got stuck and started to believe that the hole was meant for him. Not because he couldn't get out, but because he didn't believe he could. Many people are stuck just like that man because they believe things will never change. They also fail to see that persistence will deliver them. It is not your current circumstances that seal your fate. We all get stuck at some stage of our life, but it is those who have a persistent belief things will change that eventually get out.

Some people are more interested in complaining about their situation than they are in getting out of them. Sympathy might get you some attention but it will also keep you stuck. Those who believe things will never change will never see the exit sign because they're too busy looking down. Rather than looking up, because that is where our hope comes from. Life is all about phases, seasons, and one situation after the other. And they all pass, both the good and the bad times. Don't be like a worm that dies in the cocoon, because it couldn't see itself as a butterfly. If you settle for who you are, you'll no doubt stay where you are. Never settle for who you are at the cost of what you can become.

41. THE GOD CODE VS. THE DEVIL CODE

God gave me a powerful revelation about two "codes". One is from the Devil, and leads to destruction and the other from God and leads to life. Both codes incidentally have four steps that you need to be aware of. Whichever code you're obeying will have a significant impact on your life.

All temptation comes from the Devil. It doesn't come from the city you live in or the friends you hang out with. The source of all your temptations ultimately comes from the Devil. In the first step of his code, the Devil attempts to lure you in. And once you commit to the act of sin, he will accuse and condemn you. As the Bible tells us, he is the accuser of the brethren. After that in step two, the Devil's accusation, if accepted by you, becomes your self-condemnation. And with this, the Devil is out of the picture, and all fingers point to you.

In the third step of his plan, you are under submission from the Devil. The word submission means accepting the authority of another force. And because you believed his lies, you are now under his submission. And finally, because you've submitted yourself to the Devil, he will disconnect you from God. Even though all of this happens unknowingly, it doesn't change the fact that it can happen. A fish that bites a lure doesn't get let off the hook just because he didn't see it.

With the God code, it also begins with the Devil condemning you. But in the second and most crucial step of the God code, instead of listening to the enemy, you immediately turn to the Word of God. You listen to what God says about you. Never allow the Devil to accuse you but set your sights on God and this will give you hope as opposed to despair.

In the third step, you meditate on the Bible verse John 8:3 "Who the Son sets free is free indeed". And in doing so we don't focus on what we've done wrong but instead, we look to the one who can make things right. Jesus said on the cross, "It is finished".

If we are forever blaming and condemning ourselves, we will never get out of the prison we are in. But if we turn to God and repent, he will free us. Jesus did not just die to give us victory in Heaven but also on earth. It is in the freedom we get from Christ which creates a foundation that helps us from falling back into our old ways. In the final step, we reconnect with Christ. John 15:4 says "Remain in me, as I also remain in you." Being connected to Christ is not a once-off commitment; it's a daily one. Too many people take their foot off the pedal. Let's be vigilant and follow the God code so that we can live a life of victory.

42. THINK ABOUT YOUR THINKING

Experts estimate that we think between 60 000 and 80 000 thoughts per day. That's roughly an average of 2500 to 3300 thoughts per hour! Therefore it is of great importance that we think about our thinking. Being aware of our thoughts is vital in having good mental health. Because thousands of unchecked thoughts a day will eventually take its toll – especially if the bulk of those thoughts are negative.

So how does one change your daily thought-life from negative to positive? Well firstly, it needs to be intentional; otherwise, your uncontrolled thoughts will leave you vulnerable to negative thinking. Intentionally thinking positive thoughts will allow you to overcome the negative ones you have. Most people focus on the negative because of what the world feeds them. Good news hardly makes the mainstream media. And this is exactly why we need to look for good news in a world that mostly feeds us bad news. The media will tell us about a few plane crashes and forget about the overwhelming majority that lands safely. We so easily get bogged down by the unfairness of life and as a result lose all hope. But if we lose hope, we lose everything.

For our struggle is not against flesh and blood, but against the rulers, against the authorities, against the powers of this dark world and against the spiritual forces of evil in the heavenly realms.

Ephesians 6:12

Your thought life is a case of good versus evil, and all that is good comes from God, and all that is wicked comes from the Devil. Who are you lending your ear to? You will undoubtedly adopt a mindset that you study and listen to the most. Unfortunately, many spend too much time listening to the world, which causes them to adopt a negative mindset.

If we want to live a happy and fulfilling life, amid all of life's challenges, we will need to study the Word of God. This will allow us to become conscious of our thinking. And as we start to be mindful of our thoughts we can begin to change them. And as we change our thinking we will change our lives.

43. THE GRIM REAPER

It is amazing to think that from the time we get born our body begins to die. As with everything in life; nothing lasts forever. And death will no doubt come to visit us all.

Imagine being on your deathbed, in a dark room all by yourself. And as you lay there in your final hours, you hear a knock on the door. Suddenly, the door opens, and you hear footsteps. And as you look up you see the Grim Reaper. And with that, a dialogue ensues...

Reaper: "We have matters to discuss."
You: "Please don't take my life, I'm not ready yet!"
Reaper: *(Laughs)* "Take your life? You're already dead!"
You: "What do you mean?"
Reaper: "The person you were created to be, died a long time ago."

All of a sudden you're filled with bitterness, anger, and regret as you try to make sense of it all. You start punching the Reaper with tears streaming down your face. Then he grabs you and throws you back onto the bed. And the conversation continues...

Reaper: "You, it's you! You killed that person!"
You: "What do you mean it was me?"

The Reaper takes off his backpack and grabs a chair.

Reaper: "All I've ever been, and all I ever will be, is a no one and nobody. I've known and studied you ever since the day you were born. And when I saw the abilities and talents you had, I set out to do everything in my power to prevent you from becoming that person."
You: "I thought you said it was me? That I somehow caused this to happen!"
Reaper: "It was you; I merely gave you the tools to do it yourself."

You have a perplexed look on your face, as the Reaper reaches into his bag and pulls something out...

Reaper: "Remember the day when you were still a young child and believed you could conquer the world? That's the day when I gave you this thing called doubt. But your dream was big, and doubt would not do the trick. So I developed another weapon called fear. It took me many years and several attempts to sell you this one. But eventually, you bought it! But even after doubt and fear, your dream still stood. So then I pulled out my most powerful weapon called unworthiness. I had to work around the clock, but eventually, you bought it. And then you – not me – used unworthiness to kill the person God made you be. Now I will kill the person you are!"

And with that, the Reaper swung his axe and struck you in the heart, and there you are... dead. And so the question I pose to you is this: do you want to die as the person you are or the person God made you be? There are forces out there that will do anything in their power to see that you don't become who God made you be. But there are also forces that want to see you succeed. And ultimately if you die as you are instead of who God created to be... you'll only have yourself to blame.

44. TAKE ACTION

If you open up your eyes, you'll see that life presents you with many ways and means to change for the better. Sometimes it can be found in the smallest things. We find them in sermons, gestures, scripture, and so many other things.

But what good does it do, if it doesn't do any good? You know how many people read books, go to church, listen to good advice, and don't change one bit.

So faith comes from hearing, and hearing
through the word of Christ.

Romans 10:17

Remember the seed of change lies in that verse, book, talk, or advice. But it needs to be heard and read several times over so that the word can start to affect the way you live. Put what you hear into action, and you'll change. The Bible tells us faith comes by hearing and hearing. Why is hearing mentioned twice in this passage? It is because the emphasis is on repetition. Even the world's biggest sports stars never stop training, even when they become the best. They know that in order to stay the best, they have to keep on training.

So many people want the possibility of change, but they don't to put in the work. They like to know that jogging improves their health, but they don't want to go for a run. They like to know there's always someone to talk to, but they don't want to open up. Only when possibility is mixed with action will there be the potential for a miracle to happen in your life. Don't waste your life having all these opportunities to change, and then not change. Don't just listen and think about it... but take action!

45. PURPOSE

*Commit your work to the LORD, and
your plans will be established.*

Proverbs 16:3

Have you ever wondered why so many people give up on life? Just going through the motions, and slowly tiptoeing towards their grave. They think they have nothing to live for, yet they don't want to die.

Why on earth would anybody want to live, if they having nothing to live for? There are many for which life has no particular meaning, yet somehow they push on and hang in there. This is because there's something placed in all of us, something so powerful that even if you're not living purposefully, it keeps you going. Because deep down you want to live out the purpose God created you for. Everybody has a reason for being on Earth. I can say this without any fear of error because the God that made me also made you. And if he has a purpose for my life, then he has one for you too.

All things big and small created by God have a purpose.

Animals and insects were created with a purpose, and so were you! God created you in His image. Surely God didn't send you to Earth for a vacation.

So many of us go through life asking ourselves why we would even have a purpose. And if we have one... what is our purpose? They don't bother searching long enough for answers. And when they don't get answers they start to believe they don't have one. Ignore the voices in your head telling you that you have no purpose. God's voice is the only one you need to pay attention to. And if you do this you will find your reason for being.

A lion was created to hunt, and if it doesn't; it will surely die. A tree that doesn't grow its roots will fall over and die. And if you don't do what God made you for, then something in you starts to perish.

46. RESURRECTION

*When he had said this, Jesus called in a
loud voice, "Lazarus, come out!"*

John 11:43

Once upon a time, there was a man named
Johnny. And one day he walked past a graveyard and heard a voice calling him. "Johnny!
Come over here!" It was late at night, and he was rather afraid, but his curiosity got the better of him, and
he walked straight into the graveyard. The voice sur-
faced again, "Johnny, I'm over here!" And next to the
tree stood Lucifer himself. Johnny saw him and started
to tremble with fear. He shouted: "Who are you?" to
which the Devil replied, "I'm Lucifer, and I want to
show you around a bit".

Johnny was overwhelmed by the whole occasion and
tried to comprehend it all. He was very reluctant to
proceed, but his curiosity got the better of him. "Let
me show you around Johnny; I think there is a couple
of graves you'll be interested in". This statement took
Johnny by surprise, but he continued to follow Lucifer
anyway. "Look here, Johnny, remember the time they

excluded you from the football team in junior high? This is the grave where those dreams got buried. Your ambitions are dead and buried; you're not an athlete and will never be one". Lucifer smiled and told Johnny to follow him to the next grave. The audacity of Satan made Johnny furious.

"Come on, Johnny! Look at this grave. It is from the time you studied at university, but halfway through you dropped out because you didn't have what it takes. So right here I dug a hole, threw your failure in, and buried it. Now it's dead and gone; you screwed up, and you will stay a dropout!"

The Devil was on a mission and enjoying the misery on Johnny's face. "Come, Johnny! Look at this grave, remember Samantha, the mother of your children, and once upon a time, your wife? Wow! You butchered that one. I had to dig a big hole for the mess you made with this one, but it's done… your marriage is dead and buried. You're a lousy lover, and because of you it's over, and every attempt at future love and happiness is also buried here. I hope you're happy with yourself?" This all became very overwhelming for Johnny, and in a moment of desperation, he called upon the name of Jesus. And by the sound of His name, the Devil disappeared immediately.

Johnny then ran towards the exit of the graveyard, and as he approached the exit, he was called back by yet another voice. Johnny was familiar with this voice, so he turned around, and made his way back into the graveyard. He heard the voice again and started to search. The voice was coming from a little house in the distance. So Johnny quickly made his way over there, knocked on the door, and asked if he could come in...

Keep on asking, and you will receive what you ask for. Keep on seeking, and you will find. Keep on knocking, and the door will be opened to you.

Matthew 7:7

And when the door opened, Johnny saw the messiah – Jesus Christ of Nazareth. "Johnny, I saw Lucifer showing you a bunch of graves, but there was one he forgot to show you". Johnny was quiet as he stood in awe and just proceeded to follow Jesus. Then Jesus lead Johnny to an open gravesite "This, my son, is the grave where they buried me, and where many believed that I was dead and buried, but look, the grave is open, and I am alive! So many believe that this is the only open grave, yet it's not. I can also bring back to life those graves the Devil showed you! You see Johnny, bad things happen in life because we live in a fallen world. But you have to remember the grave only represents the situation, the sand that covers the grave is called unbelief. Life happens to everyone, but it's when you think that it's over, that all your future hopes and plans get buried." And in a flash, Jesus disappeared.

> *"Those things you call dead haven't yet
> had the chance to be born."*
>
> Scatman

We all have graves in life, but depending on our beliefs, our hopes and dreams can either stay dead or be resurrected.

47. COMFORTABLY UNCOMFORTABLE

All of us have so many questions in life, some of which leave us very uncomfortable. And so instead of pursuing the answers, we tend to avoid it altogether. We must not treat these questions as a burden, but rather as something that can produce growth in our lives.

Questions such as: Where am I at this stage of my life? What am I doing with my life? Why am I here? What is my purpose? Is there a God? And where am I going when I die? Most people cringe at the very thought of these questions and will shoot them down because the weight of the verdict is often too much to handle.

The sooner we answer these questions, the more purpose-driven our lives will become. Another reason people avoid these questions is that the answers are so often hard to come by. You must never allow this reality to prevent you from pursuing the answers. Yes, life has difficult answers, and likely, we will not always get answers to all of them. But if we involve God in the questions we ask then I believe He is faithful to reveal answers to us over time. A purpose-driven life is one that involves a whole bunch of questions and a furious pursuit of the answers. How will you ever fulfill your purpose on earth if you don't even ask the question?

Mostly these questions are so uncomfortable because it points out two things; it shows us how far behind we are, and how far we still need to go. And this is what scares so many people. The task seems too daunting, so most people just decide to quit altogether.

> *"The most important questions to ask are often the most uncomfortable."*

You need to realize that without answering life's big questions, it will be tough to live a meaningful life. We must take comfort in these questions because the answers give us a starting point and show us the finish line. And instead of feeling overwhelmed, we should embrace it. The price you pay for avoiding the answers will be much higher than the price you pay for asking the questions. Don't be afraid of these uncomfortable questions because ultimately you'll find comfort in them.

48. DEPENDENCY ON CHRIST

For we do not have a high priest who is unable to empathize with our weaknesses, but we have one who has been tempted in every way, just as we are--yet he did not sin.

Hebrews 4:15

Jesus was tempted in every way, just like we are tempted today. And yet He is without sin, He can do no wrong. He resisted the Devil; He didn't give in to temptation, and he was blameless. Many will be quick to point out that Jesus was God in human form; so naturally, he had the power and ability to be without sin. They'll argue that if they were God, they'd also be without sin. They make a case for why it is easy to falter and sin. And this somehow justifies them to continue living a life of sin.

"Sin is not a reason to part ways with God; it is something that shows us why we desperately need Him."

For us to be victorious we must rely on God, because when left to our own devices, we are doomed, and living a life of sin becomes inevitable. A life without God is a life that leads us down a path of destruction. We don't have to be God to resist temptation. We just need Him in our lives and in everything we do! The more you realize you need Christ, the more you'll start to depend on Him. Furthermore, we are not only human; you are not only a body. This lie will not only cause you to sin but will keep you in sin. Saying I'm only human will exclude the fact that two-thirds of you is soul and spirit. We must pay attention to and acknowledge all three parts.

Thinking you are only flesh will cause you to live a habitual life of sin. The Bible tells us to walk in the spirit. Many people think they are helpless when it comes to the temptations they face. This allows them to justify what they do, and what they are going to do. It's time that we walk in the authority of Christ, and realize that we are not subjected to sin. And that together with Jesus, we are more than conquerors!

49. NEUTRALIZE

We destroy arguments and every lofty opinion raised against the knowledge of God, and take every thought captive to obey Christ.

2 Corinthians 10:5

We all get times where we have depressing thoughts, and getting rid of them can be a real uphill battle. Then there are other times where we just accept and allow them to occupy our minds. And when this occurs we become victims of our own thinking. Instead of standing in authority and questioning the thoughts we have. If the enemy can get you to a stage where you don't question the thoughts he tempts you with, then you become putty in his hands. Many don't question these thoughts because they accept them as truth, never questioning the validity of it.

"A mind devoid of the truth will believe any lie."

Isn't it strange how negative thoughts seamlessly pop into our heads? Almost as if someone or something is deliberately trying to sabotage us. If you want to live a victorious, triumphant life, you must be intentional about what you fill your mind with. Always ask yourself, where did this thought come from? And what opposing thought can I use to counter and neutralize the one I have. Accepting these thoughts as verbatim will cause you to live a defeated life.

On the flip side, it is also important to make mention of those times when we feel good or our day is going just the way we planned. I used to think this is too good to be true; something bad is bound to happen, and it usually did. We should never apologize for feeling good or believe that it is the norm to be down in the dumps. The enemy will always tempt us with a thought that will exalt itself against the positive one we're having.

The Bible is undoubtedly the biggest weapon against the constant onslaught of the enemy. Jesus himself quoted scripture when the Devil tempted Him. He could have said anything to make the Devil go away, but Jesus instinctively knew the power of the written word. Write down and use verses you know will neutralize the negative thoughts the enemy feeds you. Make no mistake, when you're feeling down, it's never by chance, but almost always under the intention of the enemy. And if you're going to win the battle in your mind, you will have to constantly neutralize the negative thoughts that so often plague you.

50. STARVE YOURSELF

I finally got to a stage of my life where I said I don't want to live like this anymore, not so that I can become a better person but so that Jesus could make me a new one.

This means that anyone who belongs to Christ has become a new person. The old life is gone; a new life has begun!

2 Corinthians 5:17

I knew deep down that life is about more than parties and getting wasted all the time. It is also more than just the good and bad times. It is more than the wedding, graduation, and all the other milestones in our life. I simply had to refrain from doing the things that were holding me back from living a life of significance.

However, I was trapped and couldn't get out. I was trying to rid myself of the habits until God showed me I had to starve myself of the situations and circumstances that were feeding them. In addition to this, you'll be required to cut ties with people in your life; while strengthening ties with others. I stopped putting myself in environments where I felt tempted. People are going to resent you for this, but with all due respect, this is your life... not theirs. Sometimes you have to strengthen yourself in solitude – much like Jesus did in the mountains.

I looked out of my window the other day and saw a vision of a man; that man was me, the old me. There he sat on a log with what were probably his third or fourth beer and a cigarette for good measure. I thought to myself, who is that guy? Because I could hardly even recognize that man I saw. My hunger for those things is dead, and it's all because of Jesus. You shouldn't be worried about how the change will come to pass; all you have to do is remember why you want to change. Then God will take care of the how, and He will perform the miracle. Having a hunger is great, but be careful what you're hungry for. Sometimes all you need is to starve yourself, and this starvation will inevitably stir up a new hunger in you.

51. NEW DESIRES

*You grew weary in your search, but you never
gave up. Desire gave you renewed strength,
and you did not grow weary.*

Isaiah 57:10

I used to have desires which were not serving me well, nor assisting me on the path God has chosen for me. I finally came to a stage in my life where I knew I simply had to change my ways. And so I spent most of my energy trying to change and fight off my unwanted desires. But none of this was very successful. Sometimes it would work, but mostly I'd end up falling back into my old ways.

The main problem was that I was trying to do it on my own, so I asked God to intervene. Simply fighting off the old desires would not suffice; I had to replace old desires with new ones! We change, not by fighting against our old desires but rather by asking God to replace them with new ones.

These new desires will bring about effortless change that only God can bring about in you. All I did was realize I had to change and allowed God to help me. I put my trust in Him and believed He would come through for me.

Isn't it strange how many of us ask God to break the chains, and when He does, we don't thank Him? We are quick to forget how many times God has come through for us. I found myself free of my old ways but forgot that it was God who delivered me.

Be thankful in all circumstances, for this is God's will for you who belong to Christ Jesus.

1 Thessalonians 5:18

Creating a new desire will require a series of new acts; acts that are performed against the strong pull of your old desires. It will be uncomfortable in the beginning because the mind loves familiarity. But these new acts over time will breed new intent. But if your good intent stops, the old desires are likely to creep in again. Sow the seed, and God will grow the tree.

Never hesitate to celebrate... in fact, celebrate early. When I was going through this metamorphosis it resulted in fewer weekend binges, I thought to myself, "This is too good to be true". I would start doubting myself because I thought I'd mess up again and fall back into my old ways. This will happen to you too, but you need to ignore this thought at all costs! Celebrate the victory early, while you're winning, and it will undoubtedly lead to triumph. Never apologize, and just keep on affirming that the chains are broken. Celebrating early will give you the fuel to carry on and will leave less room for failure.

Now I'm on a new high because God gave me new desires. I get to live out God's plan for my life, writing books, doing talks, etc. I exchanged a case of beer and a pack of cigarettes for a life of significance – what a small price to pay. If you don't believe that you can be more, you'll hold on to the little you have. Go on your knees and ask God for new desires, then be diligent in your prayers, and He shall deliver you, Amen!

52. ALPHA GOD

In 2014, DeepMind, a UK based artificial intelligence company, designed a program called AlphaGo. This AI program was designed to beat human players at an ancient Chinese board game called Go. And to test the efficiency of AlphaGo, they opted to challenge 18-time world champion, Lee Sedol, who gladly accepted the challenge. And in 2016 a five-match series was scheduled to take place in Seoul.

Go is considered a very popular pastime in Korea, so the hype around this series turned out to be a media frenzy of note. Over 200 million people tuned in to watch the spectacle. Sedol said that this would be a 5 - 0 white-wash, in his favor. AlphaGo had beaten lesser opponents before, but surely beating Sedol would prove to be a bridge too far. The experts predicted that it would take an AI program like AlphaGo at least another ten years to challenge someone like Sedol. However, AlphaGo isn't just any program; it uses an artificial neural network, a type of deep learning method to train itself. It learns both by human and computer play and studies thousands of games, thus equipping it to make the best possible moves on the board.

There was a massive buildup to the first game of the series. Much to the surprise of many, AlphaGo won! This was a massive shock, leaving Sedol devastated while putting team AlphaGo on the front page of the local newspapers. During game two, AlphaGo made a bizarre move which left its onlookers stunned. This, however, turned out to be a stroke of genius from AlphaGo. Some called move 37, a very "creative" and "unique" advance, and ultimately paved the way for AlphaGo to win the second game. AlphaGo went on to win round three as well and left Sedol speechless. Team AlphaGo had already won the series with 2 rounds to spare. All Sedol could do was play for pride and try to perform a miracle and beat this seemingly unstoppable computer.

Match four was going right down to the wire, and just as it seemed as though AlphaGo would get the edge; Sedol made a miraculous move. An unlikely 'one in ten thousand' move, wedging his stone methodically in between that of AlphaGo's two stones. This move was dubbed "God's Touch" and proved vital in Sedol winning match four, against all odds. AlphaGo would go on to win match five and ended up winning the series 4 - 1.

Everybody marveled at the sheer brilliance of AlphaGo, and the minds that created it. People could also not stop talking about Sedol's famous move. But so many people forget to take a deeper look and trace this magnificence back to its origin. As good as the program is we must remember there's an Alpha God who created team AlphaGo. And it was also God who created the intelligent mind of Sedol. We must never forget that what is majestic was made with majesty. Try to look for the beauty amid the darkness in this world. And when you see the beauty, you will see God.

53. THE FINAL CHAPTER

*"Your circumstances do not devalue
God's promises for your life."*

After reading this book, my wish is that it will produce a great sense of hope and motivation in you for a brighter future – a future that God has designed for you. So many of us may look at our life thus far and see a slaughterhouse of failure, a graveyard full of skeletons. But that's only a part of the story. There are moments that not only determine our future but also redefine our past. May your decision to change your life, be one of those moments. The final chapter of your life has not been written yet! So with this in mind I want you to finish this book. How does your final chapter look like? You now get to write the final chapter of your life on the next page... the life God has designed for you. Amen!